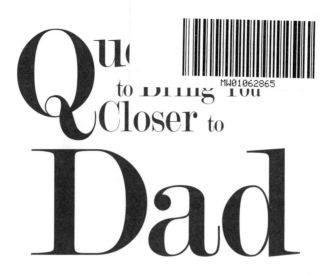

Questions to Bring You Closer to Dad

100+ Conversation Starters for Fathers and Children of Any Age!

Stuart Gustafson and Robyn Freedman Spizman

Adams Media
Avon, Massachusetts

Published by Adams Media,
an F+W Publications Company
57 Littlefield Street
Avon, MA 02322
www.adamsmedia.com

ISBN 10: 1-59869-282-8
ISBN 13: 978-1-59869-282-2

Printed in Canada.

J I H G F E D C B A

Library of Congress Cataloging-in-Publication Data
is available from the publisher.

This publication is designed to provide accurate and authoritative information with regard to the subject matter covered. It is sold with the understanding that the publisher is not engaged in rendering legal, accounting, or other professional advice. If legal advice or other expert assistance is required, the services of a competent professional person should be sought.
  —From a *Declaration of Principles* jointly adopted by a Committee of the American Bar Association and a Committee of Publishers and Associations

Many of the designations used by manufacturers and sellers to distinguish their products are claimed as trademarks. Where those designations appear in this book and Adams Media was aware of a trademark claim, the designations have been printed with initial capital letters.

This book is available at quantity discounts for bulk purchases.
For information, please call 1-800-289-0963.

From Stuart Gustafson—I wish to dedicate this book primarily to my mother, Stella, whose own personal life was deeply changed by my father's death while she was still in her prime at the age of forty-six. Her strong will and determination allowed us to continue as a family unit, when many families might have accepted the tragedy as reason for its dissolution. I also dedicate this book to all the fathers and mothers who have opened up their lives to their children, sharing their innermost thoughts and secrets to ensure that they are passed from one generation to the next. And finally, I dedicate this book to my own two children, Adrianne and Woodrow, and to my wife of thirty-two years, Darlene Smith. I love you all very much.

From Robyn Freedman Spizman—I remain eternally grateful to Stuart Gustafson, for without his vision for this book, it would not have become a reality. To my parents, Phyllis and Jack Freedman, who have shared with me the joy of the generations past and celebrated the goal of preserving the special memories we all hold near and dear to our hearts. And to my husband Willy and our children, Justin and Ali, who make my life so worthwhile and create new memories that sustain me. A special thanks to Doug and Genie Freedman, Sam and Gena Spizman, Aunt Lois, and Aunt Ramona, and to my real-life angel Bettye Storne, The Spizman Agency, Jenny Corsey, and my family and friends who grace my life with unending support and love. Plus to those family members who are no longer here and deeply missed, you will always be permanently recorded in my mind and heart.

contents

acknowledgments

The creation of a book like this is never the creation of only the people whose names are on the title page. We have been truly blessed to have the support of so many people—those who are very close to us, as well as those who responded when we asked them for some help. Thank you to Geoffrey Berwind of Bradley Communications for the encouragement and the positive reinforcement, plus the following people who contributed questions for inclusion in the book: Amanda Houston, Carrie Purdy, Cindy Casey, Connie Turnbull, Eric Spencer, Irene Anderson, John Hussar, Kelly Robert, Kimberly Barker, Lindsie Taylor, Luis Morales, Lynda Swanson, Marcy Schechter, Merla Lloyd, Mike Lyons, Patrick H. Davis, Paul Turnbull, Sharon Griggs, and Jack and Phyllis Freedman. Some of the contributions were reworded, and some of them were duplicates, but we tried to incorporate as many as possible in their original form. We are particularly grateful for the trust that they have placed in us—opening up the window so others can see inside your personal life requires a very trusting soul. We remain eternally grateful. We are also very fortunate to have the professional expertise of a fantastic agent—we extend our thanks to Meredith Bernstein for her advice and assistance.

No book can go from thoughts to final form without the professional support that we have received from all the people at Adams Media. We want to particularly thank Gary Krebs, Director of Publishing; Karen Cooper, Director of Marketing; Beth Gissinger, Director of Publicity; Paula Munier, Acquisition Editor; and Brendan O'Neill, Assistant to Paula Munier.

Harvey Mackay quote reprinted with permission from nationally syndicated columnist Harvey Mackay, author of *New York Times* number one bestseller *Swim with the Sharks Without Being Eaten Alive.*

"Foreword"

WHAT A GOOD LIFE I HAD. Sixteen years old; the summer before my senior year in high school. I would be going away to college next year, and this was to be my summer with Dad. My eldest brother, who was preparing to become an officer in the U.S. Navy, was entering his fourth year of college. My other brother had just graduated from high school, so although he was planning to stay at home and go to a local college he was technically on his own.

This was my summer. My grandfather and his wife, Hedwig, had driven out from Vero Beach, Florida, to spend a few weeks with us. I did not know them very well. My dad's family lived mostly in Ohio, but we lived in the West as my dad was in the U.S. Navy.

Life was also good at home. We were not a wealthy family, but life was comfortable. Even though Mom worked, we always had freshly ironed clothes to wear, and there was always a nutritious meal on the table. My dad had retired from the navy and had become a purchasing agent. Just the previous summer, we had taken our first vacation in many years, something we hadn't done because Dad was gone a lot when he was in the navy.

Yes, life was good.

July 19, 1964, was a typical Sunday. Grandpa and Hedwig had arrived a few days earlier, and we had all gone to Grace Lutheran Church together. After church, Dad was going to take Grandpa fishing in the Salton Sea. He and Grandpa were in the front seat of our 1962 Buick Electra, and my brother Dave and our friend Randy Gray were in the back. I have never enjoyed fishing. But if I had gone with them that day, I would have been sitting in the front seat between Dad and Grandpa.

They had been gone about an hour or so when the phone rang. I answered the phone and I heard what I remember thinking at the time was a strange question. The voice on the phone said, "This is El Centro Community Hospital. Do you know who the doctor is for David Gustafson?" I told them, but I thought it was strange that they had not asked Dad who my brother Dave's doctor was. Certainly, if Dave had been in an accident, Dad would have been able to tell them the name of our family doctor.

Mom and I immediately drove to the hospital, where our minister, Pastor Paul Harting, met us. He said there had been an accident (a word I refuse to use—it was a car crash), and that three people were dead. That was all we knew at the time. We soon learned that both Dad and Grandpa had been killed instantly when the drunk driver in the other car hit them head-on. My brother Dave and our friend Randy survived, although Dave was severely injured.

Not a day since has gone by that I have not thought of my father and grandfather and that tragic day. Over forty-two years later, I still yearn to have one more conversation with each of them.

So how does all of that relate to this book?

I expected that Dad would live forever. My father had served our country in two major wars (World War II and the Korean Conflict) and been in areas where many soldiers tragically came home in bodybags. He survived all of that.

But he did not live forever. Had I known that he was not going to live long enough to see me graduate from high school or college, or see me get married and have children—had I known all of that, I know one thing. I would have asked him a lot of questions.

When I first proposed the idea of this book to my wife Darlene, her response was so positive that I began writing immediately. She knew that this book would be good for me, as I would have to address many feelings that I had repressed during the more than forty years since my father's death. She also knew that many other people would need to address and discuss the same topics.

This book is a list of questions that I wish I had thought to ask my dad. I am sorry that I did not—I never even imagined that it would be necessary. After all, we would have discussed these important topics at some point or another later on, wouldn't we? I have shed many tears while writing these words, both here and in the pages to follow. It has been very hard for me to look at these questions and then to think what Dad might have told me in response. I really wish I knew those answers!

With the assistance of my dedicated coauthor, Robyn Freedman Spizman, who is one of the foremost gift-giving experts in the country, this book became a reality. Robyn has spent a great deal of her career writing inspirational books that help make life more memorable and meaningful, so it was natural for us to team up. We hope that this book will make a difference in your life and assist you in preserving those special memories with and about your dad.

Ah, if this book had been around back in 1963 or 1964, when my dad could have responded.

—*Stuart Gustafson*
Boise, Idaho

Part 1

How to Use this Book

"How to Use This Book"

A DAD WEARS SO MANY HATS IN LIFE. He's our encourager, philosopher, teacher, motivator, counselor, rule-maker, provider, and most often our greatest fan. We wish to congratulate you for taking an important step in life to honor him. By filling out the pages in this book, you are making an effort to let your dad know how much he means to you and how much you love him. In return, you'll also have a wealth of stories, insights, and lessons learned that reflect your father's life and the legacy he wishes to have you carry on.

If you have the luxury of sitting down with your dad, you are a very fortunate person. Life has blessed you with the opportunity to get to know your dad in even more meaningful ways that will support and comfort you for years to come. Or perhaps you are a dad, and you have decided to fill out this book yourself and later present it to your children as a loving will of sorts—we think that's absolutely wonderful. Our goal is to make sure that every dad leaves not only memories of his heartfelt love but a legacy of loving thoughts, ideas, and beliefs expressed for generations to come.

If your father is no longer alive, we hope to provide a special way to bring Dad's most special attributes and memories to light. With the help of the questions in this book, and through your family and other people who knew him, it is still possible to obtain the answers. All you have to do is make the time.

We begin with a section called "Types of Dads," which details eighteen different varieties of dads. When you find the one that best fits your dad, you can refer to the accompanying ideas for ways to begin conversations with him. We also suggest things you can do together, show you how to have "Dad radar" for things he likes, and point out his pet peeves and how to avoid them.

We organized this book to assist you in documenting the details of your father's life. Our goal is to help you provide a legacy that will forever serve as a written record. The pages following the "Types of Dads" section are divided into ten thematic parts. Each provides a thoughtful set of questions meant to ignite a conversation with your dad on the following general topics:

- On Dad's Life
- On Our Family History
- On Dad's Values
- On Marriage and Relationships
- On Dad's Dreams and Goals

- On Parenting and Children
- On Dad's Vision for His Children
- On Dad's Legacy
- Who Knows Dad Best
- Dad's Favorite Things

Before you begin, share with Dad the subject of each of these sections and the topics you'll be asking him about, and reassure him that you will be getting to each topic. While it might be difficult, it's important not to interrupt him if he goes off on a tangent. If Dad enjoys rambling on, then be prepared with knowledge of all the questions in this book and enter his stories or thoughts wherever they fit best.

To begin, start by asking one question and then recording your dad's answer in writing in this book. Conducting the questions as an interview is certainly more fun, and the answers can be written out and then transferred to this book. But if time or distance makes this impossible, there are certainly other options. You can record your conversations with Dad on tape or ask him to fill out some of the sections he might prefer to write for himself. You can also fill out his list of favorite things and then ask him for the answers, and see if your lists match.

There are several ways you can go about gathering information if your dad is no longer living. We have three suggestions:

1.   The next time there is a family gathering, pull out this book, and tell your family that you want to get some information about Dad. Read a question, and then ask, "How would Dad have answered that?" You will likely hear several responses to any one question; there might even be a few differences in the answers. That's okay. Write them all down if you can.

2.   Write out some of the questions on your own paper, and send them out to family members and friends who knew your dad. Provide some explanation about this new project you are working on. Tell them you have a lot of questions you are trying to answer as if your dad were answering them for you. Let these people know that there is no time deadline, but that you would appreciate their sending back anything they have within a month. As a courtesy, enclose a self-addressed, stamped envelope with your letter.

3.   Buy extra copies of this book. Write up a cover letter telling friends and family what you are doing. Then send two copies of the book along with your letter to family members and friends. Ask them to fill out as much as they can in one of the books and send it back to you. (Send them a prepaid envelope to make it easier.) The other book is for them to keep—they can use it to develop their own keepsake of your dad, or they could use it to begin their own journey to find out more about their own dads.

We send our best wishes to you as you begin your quest to take a closer view and inside look at the man you lovingly call "Dad."

"Types of Dads and Their Characteristics"

THERE'S A WORLD OF DADS OUT THERE, and each one is different. While every dad is different, dads do fall into categories. Each type of dad has its own characteristics, and there are some key essentials about each type that can help you. The more that you know about these characteristics, and the more that you work to understand how they apply to your dad, the better understanding you will begin to have of your dad. You will also see how he communicates and how you can communicate with him—not just a "How was your day?" talk but a deeper communication that he holds within himself.

As you read through the categories, you will probably find that there are several types that describe your dad. Generally, however, there is a single one that is central to his core—this is what truly defines him. This is what we call his central characteristic. It does not matter what season of the year it is; it does not matter if he is at work or on vacation; it does not matter if he is forty or seventy—this basic core personality trait, or central characteristic, stays with him and best describes him, day in and day out.

There are, of course, secondary characteristics that come into play at different times. He may exhibit what appears to be a different central characteristic when he is hosting a party, for example, but that is actually just a secondary characteristic that has temporarily surfaced. Deep inside, his central characteristic has not changed; he has just allowed another one to be more dominant for a short time.

The Benefits of Knowing Your Dad's Central Characteristic

- Knowing your dad's central characteristic will tell you a lot about him that you might not already know. This can also explain a lot about you—it is very likely that you have many of his tendencies. You might not want to admit certain pieces of it, but you are a lot like Dad. Now that you know this, you can see how other people see you and why they react the way that they do.
- You'll be able to talk to Dad about what interests him the most. Knowing his central characteristic gives you insight into his favorite things, and you'll find it easier to begin and hold a meaningful conversation with him. It's not just the conversations that

you can have with him, though; knowing about the things that interest Dad can also give you an indication of why certain things appeal to him, or why they bring about a reaction in him.

How many times have you asked your dad what he would like as a present for his birthday? Many times, of course, his typical answer was probably "I don't really need anything." Once you have determined his central characteristic, you will have that vision of the types of things that he likes because you will now have your "Dad radar" always switched to "on." The interesting thing is that Dad is probably not even aware that his likes (and dislikes) are so easily identified. Watch his face as you give him something that he likes: "How did you know?" is a typical response. Don't try to explain that you knew he liked this or that because his central characteristic says so. Just say that you tried to find something that you "thought he would like."

Characteristics of Dads

The following eighteen central characteristics of dads are not meant as a clinical or a psychological description of fathers. We are not clinicians or psychologists; we are people who understand the importance of learning about Dad, and we want to share our knowledge and feelings with you.

Once you have settled on that central characteristic, then you can move on to the next section: "What Your Dad's Central Characteristic Means to You." Be patient. Don't jump ahead to the next section until you have spent the time to truly understand and recognize your dad's central characteristic.

Adventurous

This type of dad does not like to be idle. He wants to be on the go—seeing new places, trying new things, and meeting new people. He will climb a mountain just to see the view from up top. He will kayak down a rushing river for the adrenaline rush. He will not typically be found sitting on the balcony reading a book while on vacation—he is out exploring the town just "to see what's there." This type of dad also is a risk taker.

Career-Driven

This type of dad is focused on nurturing a long-term working relationship in a given profession or at a particular place of employment. He is totally consumed with his work and is clearly most focused on work-related topics a majority of the time. He will do things that are aimed toward enhancing his position in that profession or at that place of employment. He is willing to make current sacrifices in return for long-term achievements.

Community-Minded

This type of dad is very involved in his local area or anything that affects his neighborhood and community. He might be on the school board, or he may participate in various community activities. In some way, he exhibits great concern for his community. This type of dad might hold an elected office in the neighborhood he lives in, and he cares about the little things that make life better for his family. He knows the difference one person can make, and he never takes a back seat when it comes to expressing his opinions and working hard to make his surroundings better.

Competitive Sports–Loving

This type of dad loves to engage in sports activities where he can play against someone else and, hopefully, win. Competition is his middle name. He may say he plays racquetball for the exercise, but he really plays it to beat his opponent and give it that ol' college try. Winning is more important than just playing; it is the primary reason that he does play, and that competitive edge is something he values. Whether it makes him feel young, or in control, or just satisfied that he has won, this type of dad loves winning. He might be a gracious winner, but he can also be a very poor loser.

Couch Potato

This type of dad does not have many activities outside his daily routine of making a living. He is generally a good provider for his family, but when he comes home at the end of the day, he does not want to do much around the house. This is not the same as the self-absorbed dad; the couch potato is essentially lazy once he gets home. This type of dad is content just hanging out in front of the television or reading the newspaper.

Difficult

This type of dad is a combination of many other types. He is the one who is not pleasant to be around for any of a set of reasons. He might be the type who wants to pick a fight (verbal or physical) no matter what the conversation is; he was probably the schoolyard bully back in elementary school; or he is the egotist who is always right, even when he is actually wrong. He will give you an excuse to dismiss his error, but he will never admit that he was wrong. This dad just might have a bad attitude all the time that could be the result of a traumatic childhood or a set of unfortunate adult experiences. He is perpetually mad at the world.

Free-Spirited

This type of dad is truly carefree. He is not concerned with results of actions (or inactions); his focus is on his current activities.

He wants to enjoy life, and he wants to live for the moment. This does not mean he takes huge risks. His attitude is that he will do what he wants to do, and if something happens as a result, so be it. He can be described as "going with the flow."

Helping Others

This type of dad is different from the service-minded dad in that he helps people learn how to help themselves. He works in the library reading to children. You will find him in rehabilitation clinics where people are learning how to walk again after surgery or accidents. You will see him volunteering his time, talents, and skills for groups like Habitat for Humanity or one of the many other community organizations. What this type of dad holds in high regard is the process of teaching someone else how to be independent or how to learn a new skill. Giving a cash donation is something this dad will do on occasion, but he really prefers to give his time and talents so that others can "learn to help themselves."

Keeps to Himself

This type of dad is generally quiet. He doesn't say much, and is hard to reach and introspective. It appears that he is ignoring you, but don't take that personally. He is "on another wavelength," and you just have to find the right way to get through to him. This dad is not unapproachable, but he doesn't give you any indication of how to get his attention. Once you do get his attention, however, he will devote his concentration to you.

Nature-Loving

This type of dad loves being outdoors. He enjoys going for walks on trails as well as uncharted paths. He likes seeing nature as it was meant to be seen, meaning that he would rather have the chance to see an animal in the wild than see the same animal in its cage at the zoo. He thinks nature is wonderful just the way it is, and he wants to see it kept that way. He might use a book to keep track of the bird species he has seen, or he just might enjoy watching any bird that comes by.

Personal Sports–Loving

This type of dad loves sports that let him relax. His favorite might be fishing, sailing, or golf. Though some people consider these sports competitive, this type of dad does them for the pure enjoyment of the sport, and he finds great relaxation and joy in them. He is happy doing them by himself or with others, just as long as the others are not competitive. He likes solitude, and these sports provide that to him, as well as a place where he can think or simply escape the life he normally lives.

Power-Driven

This type of dad needs to be recognized as someone in power and authority. It does not matter if the power is inferential, absolute, or relational—he must be perceived as the one in charge. He will do almost anything to obtain and then retain that power. An unfortunate result of his actions can be the demise of relationships, but he considers that to be collateral damage and it is not something that overly concerns him.

Scholarly

This type of dad always wants to learn. He views everything he does as a learning experience. When he travels to another country, he takes the time to study the culture and language and to visit the museums. He reads about people who have made significant contributions so he might be able to glean something from them. He has high educational aspirations for his children, as do most dads, but academic excellence and educational achievement are of especially great importance to him. As such, this dad does not take on new encounters lightly—it might take him a while to make a decision, but once he decides, he is committed to his decision.

Self-Absorbed

This type of dad is focused primarily on himself. He might give outward appearances of other characteristics, but his primary

activities are centered on himself. This is not a common characteristic, and it is one that generally results from a traumatic or very
unpleasant situation. He will not intentionally hurt people or their
feelings, but he also is not concerned if he has to "step on people"—or over them—if they are "in his way."

Service-Minded

This type of dad gives of himself in service to others because
it's the right thing to do. This service could be in the military, as
a job and a career. It might be at a religious institution where he
greets people or visits members who are in a convalescent home
or the hospital; or it might be in a local club that helps the blind or
delivers meals to the elderly. His service is a selfless giving of his
time, energy, and efforts.

Social Magnet

This type of dad is popular and charismatic in everything he
does. Whether he is hosting the party or enjoying a party as an
invited guest, people congregate around him, and he naturally
attracts others. He is at ease no matter what the function or who
is there—people want to converse with him, be around him, and
be seen with him. He can tell jokes, or he can be conversant in
the latest news; he seems to be very informed on all the latest

happenings. Called "the life of the party," he sees social gatherings as meaningful stimulation and enjoys the company of others.

Success-Driven

This type of dad is focused on being very successful in everything that he does. He might not just focus on a given career but strive to be successful at everything—at work, in investments, and in outside activities. If he takes up a hobby, he will take classes so that he can do his best, and he will spend evenings and weekends perfecting it. Whatever he does, he's going to come out a winner.

Workaholic

This type of dad must be busy all the time. Work is his middle name. Even when he is not at work, he must have several projects that he is working on to keep him happy. He hardly ever sits still. Project-oriented, he generally does not take true "downtime" vacations; he is always working on something, such as taking notes for a future project. He is more focused on being busy than on completion. Completing a project is not critical for him, though it is certainly rewarding. At the same time, this type of dad can completely dismiss one project if another project interests him more.

What Your Dad's Central Characteristic Means to You

You probably had a difficult time deciding on your dad's central characteristic. Most people will find several that appear to fit, and it takes a long time to really decide on the one that is truly the characteristic that defines their dad. Good job—you are to be congratulated for persevering through a difficult challenge.

Before we begin, there are a few generalizations that will hold true most of the time. Let's get those out in the open now so we don't have to include them for each characteristic below:

- Ways to begin conversations: Give your dad some time to relax after he comes home from work or play. You don't have to schedule time, but be respectful of his time and other obligations. Start with, "Dad, when you have a few minutes, I would like to talk with you. Is that okay?" (Of course it's okay.)

  If you are finding it difficult to get a real conversation started, suggest a safe topic to begin with, and then slowly build on it as you stretch out tangentially from the original discussion.

- Things you can do together: Focus on doing activities that allow the two of you to spend time together—that is not the same as being in the same place and doing the same thing.

- Having "Dad radar": We all give hints and ideas on things that we like and things that we dislike, and your dad is no different. When you put on your "Dad radar," you start paying attention to his likes and dislikes, his strengths and weaknesses, and you are able to tune in to his inner feelings. This does not mean you can now psychoanalyze Dad; it just means that you know more about the things he values and the things that he considers most important in his life.
- His pet peeves, and how to avoid them: Most dads do not like to be disappointed. Do not promise something (to make him happy now) if you don't think you can actually get it done.

Using Dad's Central Characteristic to Learn about Him

Now we will tell you how you can begin a conversation with him (not as straightforward as you might think), offer some ideas on activities that the two of you can do together, and give you some ideas on what you will learn when your "Dad radar" is in the "on" position. We will also tell you about some typical pet peeves for dads with each central characteristic.

While we make general observations about each type of dad, your dad has other special qualities. Take the suggestions that we give and then augment them so that they fit your dad.

Adventurous

Being busy in a different way is what makes this type of dad happy. He keeps himself occupied by seeking out new things to do. This is especially true on weekends and on vacations, but he can be adventurous in his work also.

Ways to begin conversations, and things he would like to discuss: Most papers have a section on exciting adventures. Even if it is only an article, it will cover new and exciting places to go and thrilling things to do. Ask your dad if he read that article, and what he thought of it. If your dad has been on a recent trip, ask him about it. What was it like? Were there any dangerous moments? Would he do it again? Ask him about the people he has met doing these things. Those people are probably exciting in some way, and hearing about them is certain to be a thrilling time.

Things you can do together: There are many movies of exciting adventures available. Ask your dad if he would like to watch one. He may have seen it already; if so, he might suggest a different one. If it is one he has selected, he will be really interested in it. And if you watch it with him, then you will have scored some serious points. In addition to watching a movie, you can suggest a father–son or father–daughter outing. Many adventures are more fun—and certainly safer—if there are two people instead of just one. He will likely be very excited about having you join him. Just remember, he does this because it is exciting—don't expect a leisurely stroll.

Having "Dad radar": Your radar will feed you a lot of information on what this dad likes because he likes to do a lot of things. If you want to spend some time with Dad, plan to be busy. If hiking is his passion, and he has bought some gear for the new season, tell him that you would like to go with him as he breaks in his new gear. This private time with him will afford you plenty of time to talk and find out a little more about the things he did when he was your age.

You can also have a great time with Dad by telling him that you would like to just sit down with him and talk about one of his trips. Or maybe ask him to go for a ride with you on the weekend, and use that time to talk with him.

His pet peeves, and how to avoid them: This dad's top peeve is people who are idle. Relaxing is okay, but he does not like people who sit around and do nothing. If he asks what you are doing for the weekend, do not reply with "Nothing; probably just watch some TV." A better response would be, "My calendar is flexible right now, Dad. Was there something you wanted to do? I can move things around because I would like to do something with you." If he wants to just drop by, tell him that you would love to see him, but that you are "busy until noon."

Career-Driven

A key point to remember about a career-driven dad is that he focuses on the long-term nature of situations, relationships, and so on. This means that he will not want to hear about any quick fixes or solutions that do not stand the test of time. He will sacrifice for today so he can invest in and for the future.

Ways to begin conversations, and things he would like to discuss: This type of dad is generally straightforward, so the best approach to any conversation is the direct one. Ask him why he decided to get into his profession and when he made that decision. If he is retired, ask him what was most satisfying about his career. He probably watches the evening news, usually on the same national network. Ask him about current events and the impact that they have on local and national affairs.

Things you can do together: Just because he is career driven does not mean that he might not like to go to a ballgame with you. Ask him to help you on a project—a school project or one around your house or apartment. If you are still in school, he would probably be willing to talk to your class about his career.

Having "Dad radar": Your radar should easily detect the strong focus that this type of dad has in everything he does, especially toward his job. He likes to stay current in his areas of interest, and these should be very apparent to you.

This dad might like a copy of the recent bestselling business book or the chance to attend a local seminar; you can enhance the experience by buying two tickets—one for him and one for you. That way, you'll spend some valuable time with your dad (and you might even gain something from the seminar).

If your "Dad radar" tells you that he would like a wooden deck in the backyard, do more than just offering to help him. Buy him a book about how to build a deck, and insert a note that says what you will do to help. You might even point out a particular style that your radar has told you he would like. If he has already determined the style, and he knows what to do, tell him that you will stain the deck when it is finished.

His pet peeves, and how to avoid them: He is not a proponent of major changes, which means he really likes the status quo. Therefore, don't tell him in advance that you are going to change your school, college major, employer, or profession. Do what you have to do, and don't tell him. If he finds out later, tell him that you didn't think he would be interested. Don't talk about his employer's competitors—he probably doesn't view them as worthy of being called competitors.

Community-Minded

This type of dad has a great awareness and feeling for his neighbors and friends (who are really the same to him). The community is an important part of him—it defines who he is and so he takes great pride in it. He considers the community to be his home.

Ways to begin conversations, and things he would like to discuss: The local newspaper and local TV news stations are great sources of material for you. There are bound to be several items each day concerning happenings in the local area. Start by asking your dad's opinion of this thing or that. While it is easy to focus on the negative, he prefers the positive things that are happening. Talk to him about the center for the homeless that just opened or the increase in school funding for elementary education.

Things you can do together: You will make your dad very happy by asking if he would like to attend a local event with you. He might also appreciate your helping him as he rakes the leaves from a neighbor's lawn. Because of his interest in the community, he also cares about how his house looks. If you know that he is going to take on a home improvement project, ask him if he would like some help. He will say yes.

Having "Dad radar": It's a good thing that your radar doesn't have to keep track of this dad, because he spends a lot of his time doing things in and around his community. He likes the neighborhood to be nice, but he probably spends so much time helping others that he doesn't always have time to complete the projects around his house. Was he talking about painting the eaves this year? You can print up a set of coupons for "eight hours of expert eaves painting" for him.

Consider giving something in his name to the library, for example. Or perhaps you can give items to an organization that helps others—something like a Boys and Girls Club, or a senior center. The recipients will get something they really want, and you will have performed some community service in your dad's name. If you have the time, you might ask your dad if the two of you can perform some community service together. These times together will have special meaning for both you and Dad.

His pet peeves, and how to avoid them: This dad doesn't like waste. Don't let him see you wasting time or energy. He also doesn't like to see litter. He doesn't like politicians who are nothing more than talking heads. He expects you to back up your words with actions. Don't talk about the wasted time and money that's spent on community activities. Maybe they are not very efficient, but your dad considers them very important activities.

Competitive Sports–Loving

This type of dad will know more about what's in today's sports section than on the front page or local section. He is very active, and he will likely have a fairly strict schedule for his exercise, so you can't just plan on dropping in. If the two of you share a common routine (afternoon jogging, for example), you might be able to get some of his time by stopping by in your jogging clothes.

Ways to begin conversations, and things he would like to discuss: If you also like sports, just go to the latest headline. Whether it is Tiger Woods winning another golf tournament or Kobe Bryant leading the Lakers to another NBA title, you'll find no shortage of easy entries into a conversation. But he likes to talk about other things; starting a conversation about weather changes (getting warmer, not colder) is also an idea. He will also like to debate a current topic, but beware. He will want to win!

Things you can do together: Almost any sporting event is a natural for the two of you (if you like sports). But don't suggest a sport that he doesn't like. You can challenge him to a game of some kind, but be prepared for a tough opponent. He would even enjoy an evening with you watching an event on TV. While he does not profess to like public speaking events, he will go with you if the speakers are high-profile competitors—whether in sports, business, or politics.

Having "Dad radar": This dad will send strong radar signals about the things he likes, and sports will generally play a very significant role. As you stay tuned in to your "Dad radar," you will see that you have many opportunities to spend time with him—so long as you like sports! If you challenge him to a game, be prepared to face a very intense competitor. While he is playing his hardest to trounce you, you have the rare opportunity to see your dad for who he truly is. If he is going to swear, you will hear one or two words that you never heard him say at home. The one thing you won't see is "quit"; that word is not in his vocabulary.

Another thing that your "Dad radar" might pick up is that he likes to attend high-energy sports events. If you live near a sports city, get a pair of tickets to a hometown game. Even though you are observing and not participating, the excitement of the event will allow him to open up to you a little more.

His pet peeves, and how to avoid them: Because he is so competitive, he expects others to have an inner drive. He knows this is an unrealistic expectation, but that does not change the fact that he doesn't like "lazy" people. He will not call you that to your face, but you can see it in his expressions or hear it in his voice. Show him that you have a competitive spirit, even if it is not as strong as his. This spirit can be in making good grades or in taking on challenges in extracurricular activities.

Couch Potato

It is not easy to relate to this type of dad unless you plop down in front of the TV. He is a good man, but he does not want to do much after work. He considers this his right since he provides for his family and is a good dad. It can be a challenge to get close to him because he is not very social, and he does not have many close friends. You can use this to your advantage because you will not have much competition for his time and attention.

Ways to begin conversations, and things he would like to discuss: You can ask this dad about TV programs because he probably watches most of the prime-time shows and sports programs. A simple "What's on tonight, Dad?" will result in a comprehensive listing that compares to the *TV Guide* channel. Given that he does not have many outside interests, finding a mutual conversation topic other than television can be difficult.

Things you can do together: Watch TV! This type of dad might have some activities that he likes to do, but these are generally not obvious. By nature, he is not a very social person, so any activities he does enjoy are going to be where he does not have to interact with very many people. He might like to work on his car (only his, not any others in the family), and so you could offer some assistance. Ask him if he needs any help first before just jumping in. It is possible that there is an activity that you enjoy—and he might also—but he has not been exposed to it. It is okay to suggest it, just don't be surprised if he is not interested.

Having "Dad radar": This dad's interests are limited, but you still need to be aware of the signals you receive on your radar. What you will find is that his likes vary depending on the season. For example, in the fall, he will prefer to just stay inside (and possibly watch football), but in the summer he might enjoy taking the boat to the lake for a lazy day. Once you determine what he likes at the moment, try to find the right time to be there with him.

If you want to get something for him, find something that accompanies his current set of likes. That could be something for the boat, a new recliner, and so on. If he has a favorite sports team, maybe you can get a signature item from that team.

His pet peeves, and how to avoid them: He does not like to be called lazy, even though he generally is. He will say that he works hard, and so he needs to relax and be ready for the next day. It is hard to fault him for that because he is a good provider for his family. He probably has a favorite place to sit—stay away from that seat. He also does not like to be bothered while he is intently watching one of his favorite shows.

Difficult

You will ask yourself many times if it is even worth trying to make any contact with this type of dad, let alone struggle to build or hold on to a relationship with him. His combative nature puts up barriers that are difficult to cross. Keep in mind that he is the only one you call "Dad." So while the efforts can be huge and largely met with resistance, avoidance, or apathy, don't give up. He is a tougher figure to get through to than any of the other dads we have described, but he is the one who needs it the most. Your ability to relate to him, to let him know that you care about him and that you love him—these could be the triggers to help him begin the slow transformation from this central characteristic to another one.

Ways to begin conversations, and things he would like to discuss: There are no standard ways to begin a discussion with this type of dad. His volatile nature makes it difficult to invade his personal space. One approach is a humble opening like, "Hi, Dad. I've got a couple things I would like to talk to you about. Do you have some time?" This lets him know that you are not in an attacking mode. (He may say he is aggressive because he is used to people attacking him.) Unless there is some bad blood between the two of you, he will probably warm up to you after a light conversation. You will have to let him guide your talks so he knows that it is safe to talk with you. Once you are able to engage with him for longer conversations, you can start to introduce some new topics, but you will need to exercise restraint and patience.

Things you can do together: You will have to be very open to doing almost anything or to doing absolutely nothing to be with your dad. Getting him to talk with you (rather than at you) is a significant first step. Finding things that he wants to do will be a slow process that requires perseverance and a lot of patience. If you know that there are certain things he likes to do, you might suggest one of them. Avoid any "dangerous" activities—ones where your dad is exposed to situations where his bad side comes out.

Having "Dad radar": Even though your dad is very temperamental, it is still important for you to keep your radar turned "on." There will be times when he is receptive to talking with you—take advantage of those times! If there is a particular task around the house that he really doesn't like doing, maybe you can do it for him. It not only gives you a chance to be around him, but it also removes a source of his frustration.

His pet peeves, and how to avoid them: Do not criticize this type of dad, even though it maybe be justified. His response might be that he is that way because of something that he can blame on someone or something else.

Free-Spirited

This type of dad is probably the easiest to relate to, as long as you are willing to be flexible and adaptive. He is open to so many things that you can just wait for the right moment. He likes spontaneity, which means that you can suggest almost anything to him at the last moment.

Ways to begin conversations, and things he would like to discuss: This dad will talk about almost anything, with an emphasis on "almost." He does not care much for politics, unless the topic impacts the local environment. There are probably many events that interest him, and these make great conversation starters. He will also talk with you about some of his recent activities. If there is anything sitting around that is indicative of something he has done (a souvenir, a photo, and so on), ask him about it and what the activity was like. He will freely talk about it.

Things you can do together: This dad will do almost anything with you, even if it is a spur-of-the-moment activity. He likes doing things, and this gives you a lot of freedom for different activities that you can suggest to him that you both do. A simple approach is to just ask him what he would like to do. He will give you an honest answer. If you do not have a lot of time, you can suggest a short walk around the block or even a quick game of cards.

Having "Dad radar": This dad likes a lot of activities, and your radar will be telling you many things. Because of his spontaneity, you have to stay tuned in to know what his current preferences include. If you are willing to do almost anything at the drop of a hat, then be prepared to have a great time with your dad.

If you want to do something for him for a birthday or other special time, you can offer to take him on an adventurous hike, take him golfing when the weather is nice, or buy a subscription to any one of the magazines that covers his activities; or a gift certificate for dinner at a casual yet eclectic restaurant.

He probably has a trip or an outing planned; ask him what he is doing next. Then ask him if there is something special that you could get for him to make it even more enjoyable. He doesn't always need something tangible, so an alternative would be to pick up the tab for a sporting event that you two attend.

His pet peeves, and how to avoid them: This dad does not stick to normal activities, nor does he like to be considered part of the majority. He does what he wants, when he wants. His primary pet peeve is people who do not stray outside the lines. Don't suggest a follow-the-crowd activity or something very structured (such as a guided tour). He also doesn't plan many things far into the future. He might like the activity once it gets closer, but he doesn't want to commit to it too early.

Helping Others

Seeing someone learn a new skill is a thrill that will never cease to excite this dad. He feels that most people want to be able to do things for themselves rather than have things given to them. His service to others is in a learning mode—helping them learn to help themselves. This takes many forms, but the constant is that Dad is there, patiently working with someone until the skill is learned.

Ways to begin conversations, and things he would like to discuss: This dad is happy to talk about the places where he volunteers his time. Beginning a conversation with him can be as simple as, "Dad, tell me a little about the people you help. What is it like? What are the people like?" If you want to see a smile come across his face, ask him to talk about someone whose life has been changed by his efforts. He will play down his role. He will say he did just a small part in it—that the greatest contribution came from the person themself. He will tell you about the joy that he sees in these people as they have learned to help themselves.

Things you can do together: While it might seem that working in the same activities as your dad is an automatic choice, this is not necessarily true. Your dad will appreciate your help, but he is more concerned with long-term solutions. This depends, of course, on what the "work" is. Anything you do in the construction of a

Habitat for Humanity house will be a tremendous contribution. Another way you two can work together might be to visit garage sales for good books that can acquired cheaply, and then have him give those books to people who are learning to read. This dad is probably a quiet dad, and so you two might be able to spend some time together going for a walk along a pleasant pathway.

Having "Dad radar": He is bound to have some personal things he likes, but his priority is others. Consider something that he uses in his work with others. Maybe it is books that he gives to new readers. Maybe he can use a new toolbelt or a hammer for building that Habitat for Humanity home. Given that he thinks more of others than himself, he would appreciate something that is given to others in his name. Actually, you don't even have to do it in his name, as he doesn't need the recognition. Just knowing that you have given to a cause that he likes will make him happy. Does he like to read? Do the two of you like a particular author? If so, sit down with him to discuss that author's latest book.

His pet peeves, and how to avoid them: This type of dad definitely does not like people who have the ability but not the drive. He spends time with people who are trying to improve their lives, and he does not want to be around people who waste away opportunities.

Keeps to Himself

You might wonder sometimes if this man is your dad or if he is just someone else who looks like him. He is not the easiest person to get through to, but deep down inside he is still Dad, and he still loves you. Patience on your part is the key to being able to strike up a conversation with him. The wait is worth it because he will focus on you once you have his attention.

Ways to begin conversations, and things he would like to discuss: A simple approach is the best way to open the dialogue; something like, "Hi, Dad. Gee, it's nice to see you." This is a nonthreatening opening that does not require him to open up and feel vulnerable. You can begin to move to topics of slightly more substance as he starts to feel more comfortable with the small talk. He will say things that give you openings on topics that he is comfortable discussing. You might have some areas from previous discussions that you know you can talk about, and these can be the safe topics.

Things you can do together: You will find that your dad feels more comfortable in areas that are familiar to him. His inward nature means that he does not typically like to venture out into new areas, to be in crowded areas, or to participate in activities that require his active involvement. Unless you know some activities to suggest, ask him what he would like to do. While he is a mystery to most people, he will open up to you. Take advantage of the times you have with Dad; they are important to him also even though he will not openly express those feelings to you.

Having "Dad radar": Your dad will not openly tell you the things that he likes, so you need to keep your radar finely tuned. He is not an open person by nature, but he will talk about certain things in a very general and impersonal manner. You need to have your antennae on at full strength to receive and process this information.

He is probably an avid reader, but his preferences may be difficult to determine. Listen to him carefully—he gives out the information you need; you just have to catch on to the subtleties.

Your dad is not flashy, so anything you get for him must be discreet and subdued. Small personal items that allow him to see the relationship with you are truly valued by him, and they also allow you to have some personal time with him.

His pet peeves, and how to avoid them: You already know that Dad doesn't like any attention brought to him or to anything he has done. He might be a wealthy philanthropist who does not want any recognition for his charity, or he might be a quiet person who does not want to be in any spotlights. Accept him for who he is. If you want to make a donation on his behalf, make it either as an anonymous donation or in honor of a loved one.

Nature-Loving

It is safe to say that this dad has several bird feeders. He loves nature and the things that belong to nature—the trees, the animals, the sounds, and even the quiet of nature. This type of dad would prefer to watch a show on the plains of Africa than the Super Bowl. He feels at peace with nature, and he considers it natural to go into the unspoiled areas of forests, meadows, and hills.

Ways to begin conversations, and things he would like to discuss: Ask him if he saw the news story on the migrating birds. Make sure you did, because it is possible that he was in the story or contributed to it. If you recently saw a beautiful animal in your yard, tell him about it. He might have a story about it, and tell you what it means ("Cold weather is on the way," for example). If he is the type who will take vacations to go observe nature, ask him about a recent trip. Why did he pick that particular one? What was the best part about it? If you are watching a nature show or movie, ask him to scientifically identify as many species as he can.

Things you can do together: Take a hike! Ask him where he would like to go; even just a nice casual walk through nature can be nice. He has at least a dozen places listed in his brain where he wants to go. He is just looking for an excuse—and a companion—to go. He will also like going to the outdoor exposition at a convention center or fairgrounds. He might even like to go to the botanical gardens. Just being in nature makes him happy.

Having "Dad radar": Pictures are not a top priority with this type of dad. Your radar tells you that he would prefer to see a century flower bloom once than to have a dozen pictures of it. What this means is that if you want to buy something, you will have to be very careful in your selection. Given the things that he likes, you don't have to spend a lot of money.

If the local garden society is sponsoring a nature walk, buy some tickets for him. Go with him and smell the roses. You could even buy tickets in his name and donate them to a nursing home. If he has talked about a trip he would like to take "because they won't bloom like this for another ten years," offer to pay for a certain part of the trip. The trip will mean even more because you have recognized it as something that he liked.

His pet peeves, and how to avoid them: Did you notice the look he gave you when you casually dropped a piece of trash as you were walking? When you carelessly throw something into an area that belongs to nature, you're essentially telling him that his ideals are not worth anything. That hurts him. Respect nature in the same way that you respect people. Remember, he loves you no matter what you do—give him the respect that he deserves for who he is.

Personal Sports–Loving

Even though this type of dad likes relaxing activities, he still might be very focused when it comes to work around the house. Don't mistake his easygoing behavior while fishing for a laid-back attitude in general. He likes being by himself, but he welcomes your company as long as you respect his desire for a peaceful setting.

Ways to begin conversations, and things he would like to discuss: This type of dad also likes sports, but he likes them for different reasons. Remember, he likes the "quieter side" of sports. You can start a conversation by talking about the sports that he likes. If he likes fishing, ask him if he saw the news article on the recent run of bass in the lake, or salmon down the river. You can also start by asking, "Dad, tell me what it is like when you are out there by yourself. How does it feel? What do you think about?"

Things you can do together: Anything that your dad likes to do, you can join him. But it needs to be a peaceful activity. When you go with him, make sure that your attitude and temper are in check. He is there for the enjoyment; don't ruin it for him if the fish breaks your line, or if you hit the ball into a pond. He will also enjoy watching his favorite sports on TV. Because his general nature is to like peaceful activities, you can suggest a car ride on a nice day.

Having "Dad radar": Your "Dad radar" will tell you that he likes things that are quiet. These can be things related to his favorite sport, or they can just be doing other things that are not high energy. Take him golfing and pay for both of you. Just because he prefers golf over racquetball does not mean that he is not competitive. When you invite him, hand him a sleeve of balls with a note attached that says, "Glad we're playing golf together. Perhaps these can help you." Get ready for a laugh and some tough competition. If he likes fishing, put a new lure inside a card, and tell him that you would like to take him fishing whenever he has some free time. Regardless of what your radar tells you that he likes, make sure that your mind is clutter-free so you can enjoy these times with your dad. The same holds if the two of you go to dinner at a relaxing restaurant. Use the time together to learn a little more about him by listening to what he says, and how he says it. Spend most of the time listening and just enjoying being able to have some quiet time with Dad.

His pet peeves, and how to avoid them: This dad isn't a fan of raucous activities, so don't turn the TV to a boisterous program. When you two play golf, don't be loud or curse when you make a bad shot. He likes the peaceful side of sports; unfortunately, there are many who don't. He will seem like a loner at times because he does not have to be surrounded by noise; don't turn on the radio or TV just to have something on. He likes the quiet.

Power-Driven

This type is typically the one who is in control of any situation. This is certainly a very natural position for the father–offspring relationship. You have two choices: remain in the subservient role, or find activities that aren't threatening to his power base.

Ways to begin conversations, and things he would like to discuss: This type of dad is used to having people defer to him; you don't have to do that. You can start a conversation with, "Dad, I have something I need (or want) to discuss. Do you have some time?" He will typically say yes because he relishes the time with you. Because of his drive for power, this dad loves Type-A personality discussions. He will talk about political hot topics, business news items, and sports (only the ones he likes).

Things you can do together: You will make super points with your dad by getting tickets to a high-profile event. For example, let's say the governor is hosting a luncheon on a topic that your dad can relate to. He will tell people how he had lunch with the governor and that you arranged it. (Your dad likes to drop names.) Other things you can do together include watching shows that feature "power people"—shows such as *The Apprentice* are a must for him. He will also enjoy games that one person can dominate and win, such as Monopoly, chess, and card games.

Having "Dad radar": Knowing that this type of dad likes to be in a position of power actually gives you a base of strength. For example, when you get him those tickets to that high-profile event, you will be setting the stage for a very meaningful conversation with your dad. That conversation could be before, during, or after the event—and it does not have to be limited to just once.

This type of dad does not spend a lot of time reading (he is too busy being "powerful"). But he would probably read a top-selling book. If you are not sure which one, buy a gift certificate and include a list of the current top-selling business books.

Besides being too busy to do much reading, he is also too busy to do much shopping—even though he likes to wear nice clothes. Tell him that you want to take him shopping just like he or your mom did for you when you were younger. This time, however, you and the sales clerks are going to pick out the clothes for him.

His pet peeves, and how to avoid them: This dad does not like underachievers. Because he is so driven himself, it's hard for him to tolerate those who do not fully apply the talents they have. It is hard for you to live up to his standards, but all he really wants is for you to live up to "your abilities." Don't criticize people who have made it on their own. You might consider them lucky, but he feels that anyone can "make it" if they try hard enough.

Scholarly

"What have you learned today?" would be an appropriate motto for this dad. He feels that there is something to be learned in everything you do, and this can be a little bit of a challenge at times. You might want to do something "just for fun," but Dad will turn it into a learning exercise. He expects great things from you academically, but that's because he knows you are capable of outstanding accomplishments.

Ways to begin conversations, and things he would like to discuss: Start by talking about anything educational. This could be something you read in the paper about the local school system or his alma mater. If you are in school, or contemplating going back to school, your dad will love to talk about this; he will probably also have plenty of advice for you.

If he has been on a recent trip, ask him about it. Did he have time to go to any museums? What were his favorite parts of the sights he saw? Ask him to tell you how he incorporates learning into his daily work life. He might even have a few suggestions for you.

Things you can do together: He will probably like going to a lecture or discussion about anything that involves learning. The subject is not as important as the setting. If the two of you have similar aptitudes, you might even be able to work together in a mentoring or tutoring program. The two of you could also give a course (some are as short as one night) on something that the two of you enjoy.

Having "Dad radar": Is there a certain newspaper or magazine that your dad likes? You could get a subscription for him and then sit down and talk with him about it. He will be surprised that you knew, but you don't need to tell him about your radar.

Your radar probably also tells you that he is an avid reader. What genre does he like? Ask your local bookseller for a recommendation, and then get it for him.

This dad is probably involved with his alumni association(s). Ask him about his alma mater. Why did he select that school? What did he like about it? If he has thought of attending his college homecoming, tell him you would like to pay for his dinner at the president's table. Watch the look on his face—it will be one of great joy.

His pet peeves, and how to avoid them: He feels that almost everyone can achieve their goals by continuing to learn. He may feel that you have potential that is not being fully utilized (what parent doesn't?). If you are not planning to further your education (after high school, college, or even a master's), tell him that you are going down a different path right now.

Self-Absorbed

Don't be surprised to discover that this dad does not have many close friends. After all, who wants to be around someone who cares primarily about himself and not others? He might tell you that he has to take care of himself because no one else is watching out for him. This is a defense mechanism that is difficult to overcome; you have to show him that you are not a threat to him.

Ways to begin conversations, and things he would like to discuss: You might have to get permission to talk with this dad. It is not that he does not want to talk with you; rather, he feels the need to have a conversation about him, not with him. The way to start this conversation is to compliment him on something recent. Perhaps his name was in the paper, or you heard of an accomplishment of his at work—use that as your icebreaker. He will usually take that entrance and begin talking.

He will want to talk about things he has done, a tendency that might make you a little uneasy. As you have more of these conversations with him, you can probably begin to expand the subject matter a little at a time. It will be a slow process, but one that is worth the extra effort.

Things you can do together: Finding good activities is actually easier than talking with this dad. Find out what he likes to do, and then offer to do it with him. Be ready for his penchant to extol his own prowess. If he is giving a talk, attend and tell him how good it was (he already knows that, but he will like hearing it from you).

Having "Dad radar": Your radar does not have to be very strong to know what this dad likes. He likes almost anything that makes him look good. He may be into status items, such as name-brand clothing or accessories. If you want to get something for him, it will be all that much better if the name is prominently displayed.

You can also make a donation in his name to a charity or other public activity. If the local public radio station is having a fundraiser, wait until they are announcing names on the radio. Call in and make a pledge in his name, and when his name is announced on the radio as supporter of the station, his ego will get a boost.

Knowing this dad's likes will also let you know when he might be more receptive to an open conversation with you.

His pet peeves, and how to avoid them: Because of his self-centered nature, this dad prefers to have the attention on himself. Chief among his dislikes are public praise for other people and downplaying the importance or value of things he has done. You have to be careful of how you phrase your remarks when he asks a question, especially if it somehow relates to him.

Service-Minded

Giving his time, skills, and energy so others benefit is what defines this type of dad. He could write a check, but he gets more satisfaction in the giving of himself. He is not focused on just one worthwhile organization; he will give his services to many groups. He wishes he had more time so he could give to more organizations.

Ways to begin conversations, and things he would like to discuss: There are bound to be newspaper articles about various local service organizations. Read one or two, and ask your dad about them. Has he done any work with them? Ask him what it was that gave him the desire to help others. Ask him to describe the satisfaction he gets out of it. If he was (or is) in the military, ask him about his motivation to join the service. Why that particular branch? What are some of the most memorable events?

Things you can do together: Volunteer, volunteer, volunteer. There is always a need for volunteers to work at food banks, homeless shelters, public TV activities, or charity events. All you have to do is to read the paper, or you can call a local TV station and ask what charity event or public service agency needs help. Working at one of these places alongside your dad will give you both a great sense of contribution, and the two of you will also have plenty of memories for discussing later.

Having "Dad radar": Here is another area where your "Dad radar" will tell you that the things he likes are not "things" for himself, but for others. Since his service to others includes not only his time but also his contributions, you can follow suit and either spend time with him or give a donation to someone else (nursing homes, crisis centers, elementary schools, or a religious organization). You can also give a donation to one of your dad's favorite charities in honor of him. Call the organization, and ask them what is high on their list of immediate needs. Get that item, and then drop it off with a note saying, "This is in honor of a man of whom I am really proud—my dad." Of course, you want to let them know who your dad is. If your radar tells you that Dad might like reading books about philanthropists and other giving people, get him a book on a particular person he likes.

His pet peeves, and how to avoid them: This dad does not like any rhetoric about how people need to be able to take care of themselves. While this might be true in some situations, your dad also recognizes that there are many circumstances where people are in unfortunate situations, and they need help. He also does not require recognition for his services, and he does not think highly of those who do. He thinks people should do good deeds because it is the right thing to do, rather than because of any recognition they receive.

Social Magnet

You will never see a stranger when you are with this type of dad. He knows many people, and he is very likeable. He likes to be around others, and he is stimulated by the buzz of an energetic party. You will be able to see the excitement in his eyes when there is a lot going on—he wants to participate in each discussion because they all interest him.

Ways to begin conversations, and things he would like to discuss: This dad is current on things that matter, whether they are in politics, business, local affairs, health, the social scene, ecology, or even sporting events. Don't start by asking, "Did you see" or "Did you hear that . . . ?" Instead, begin with "Dad, I saw in the news that . . . What do you make of it?" Or, "What do you think of the latest report from. . . . ?" If he has recently attended some event, ask him about it. Who was there? What were the highlights?

Things you can do together: This dad is at ease anywhere he goes. The two of you can go for a stroll downtown (careful, though, because he will run into many people he knows). You could visit some art galleries or go to a concert—probably not a rock concert, but you could ask him! He has many other interests, and it should be easy to find something that would fit in with them. It might be a stretch, but the two of you could go to a comedy club for amateur night.

Having "Dad radar": This dad has so many likes that your radar is constantly pinging you with new ideas. He likes to go to new places, such as the opening of a new art gallery. He might be busier talking with people than looking at the art. Buy your dad a small item that will remind him of your time together. Write a brief note to give him with the item.

Your radar will tell you that he likes things that make him look better. If you get him something, make sure that it is the best! Does he need new cufflinks? If he likes to barbeque, buy him a new set of utensils. If he asks, "Why?" say, "I know how much you like to entertain, and I thought you could use a new set." Along with a "Thanks," you might even get a hug.

If you want to really surprise him—and have some captive time with him—get in the car with him and tell him to drive to the car wash. When you get there, hand him a book of car wash certificates. Not only will he end up with a clean car, but also you will now have many opportunities to start a nice conversation.

His pet peeves, and how to avoid them: This dad is fairly laid back, so he does not have a standard set of pet peeves. But since you know him, you should know what his particular ones are. He might be a neat freak; if so, then don't leave a mess lying around. If he really likes to tell jokes, do not—repeat, *do not*—spoil his jokes even if you have heard them dozens of times.

Success-Driven

Anything you do with this type of dad must be targeted to his success. This does not mean that you have to lose—a win-win situation will be an optimal one.

Ways to begin conversations, and things he would like to discuss: This type of dad will want to talk about successful people, what they have done to be successful, and what he is doing to be successful. You can talk about what you are doing toward your own success; in fact, he will view your success as a piece of his own.

Things you can do together: You can do almost anything with this type of dad as long as there is some activity involved. He will appreciate going to a sporting event, to concerts, and to museums; he will even go to an interesting lecture with you. This dad wants to be current, which means the two of you could listen to objective and informative newscasts together. Your dad would also enjoy going to one of your alma mater's events. He is proud of what you have accomplished!

Having "Dad radar": This type of dad likes things that are associated with success. This means that he likes to dress well and be recognized as being successful.

As you tune in to this and can observe the type of clothing he wears, you can buy him something like a fashionable necktie that accentuates many dress shirts. Contrary to popular opinion, successful dads like receiving a nice tie.

Your radar will indicate whether he tends toward the trendy or the traditional. Don't try to push him into a fashion that he doesn't like. If you want to get something else in his wardrobe, consider what colors he likes. A more formal dad will appreciate a personalized set of cufflinks. Consider ways to add sentimentality to any gift by engraving it. If your radar tells you that he likes signature items, look for something that is different. Then you can add a little note saying that you can't wait to tell him the story behind it.

Because of his success, this dad will like it when you take him to lunch at a new restaurant. Meet the maitre d' and then introduce Dad. He will be very impressed, and it will also show him that his success has been passed down to you.

You can also recognize his success by obtaining an author-signed book that he would enjoy reading. Include a note that says that you would like to discuss it with him after you both have read it.

His pet peeves, and how to avoid them: He does not like failure or when people accept failure as something natural. Do not make excuses if something does not go the right way. Because he is driven by success, he does not like idle time.

Workaholic

It appears that this type of dad is always busy, so you will have to be a little more aggressive to get his time and attention. He will make the time for you, although it might appear that you are interrupting him. Once you have his attention, make good use of the time—he considers it very valuable.

Ways to begin conversations, and things he would like to discuss: Although he will appear to be busy all the time, you can approach him with, "Dad, do you have a few minutes?" He might appear to be ignoring you, but he is actually completing a thought so he can give you his undivided attention. He likes to talk about his projects, so if you show interest in one, he will explain what he is doing and why. When you do have his attention, ask him where he learned his work ethic. No one has probably asked him that before, and that question might allow him to open up a little more to you.

Things you can do together: Given that he is always working, you might ask if he would like help on a project. Maybe you can help prune the fruit trees (or pick up the cut branches). He will appreciate the help, and this also gives you the opportunity to have a one-on-one conversation. It is difficult for him to make spur-of-the-moment plans because he is so busy. But if you check a week ahead of time, he might be open to attending an event with you.

Having "Dad radar": This type of dad can always use more time, but there are still only twenty-four hours in a day. One way to spend valuable time with him and to learn more about him is to offer to help him on a project around the house.

Pay close attention to your "Dad radar" during these times with him. Given that he is typically too busy to do much communicating, he will be more open to discussing most things when you two are working together. Use these opportunities to ask him a few questions about his childhood, what his early dreams were, and what his key aspirations are. Along the way you just might pick up some ideas—hints or direct statements—on some items that he would like. It might be a new tool or CD. Wrap one of those items with a "Just because . . ." card the next time you see him. He will be pleasantly surprised that you knew what he liked.

His pet peeves, and how to avoid them: He does not like wasted time, his or yours. Don't tell him about some project you started and then let lie around (he does the same thing, but he calls it a reprioritization). He does not like idle chitchat; conversations, for him, need a meaning. While he might not appear to be extremely organized, in his mind he knows where everything is, and everything he needs to do—*do not* try to organize his work bench or straighten up his study.

Part 2
Questions
to Ask
Your Dad

"Questions to Ask Your Dad"

Now that you know so much about Dad—his central characteristic, his likes, his pet peeves—you will be able to approach the following questions with more ease and comfort. You now know why you want to ask these questions and why they are important. It is not that the questions themselves are important. Instead, what matters is that the answers you get from him will add to the reservoir—that body of knowledge—that tells you about Dad. You might think you already know him, but you will be surprised at how much more you learn about him once you start to talk with him about his childhood, his dreams and goals, and so on.

This is not a notebook to fill out just so it is finished once you have written something on every page. There are no grades, and no one is going to evaluate what you have done (or not done) when you are finished. The only one who will know how well you did is you. What you are doing is gathering information to preserve your dad's legacy today so you will have no regrets tomorrow. We don't know how much time we will have with our dads, so it is imperative that we gather and record as much as we can now—while we can. If this indicates a sense of urgency, then you have gotten the message. Don't wait to talk with Dad—get started immediately!

In case you need a reminder on how to ask the questions, turn to the earlier section "How to Use This Book." There, we gave you some tips on how to start the conversations with Dad; we also gave you three ways to gather the same information if your dad is deceased. That section is a good refresher to read any time that you have set the book down for a while before picking it back up to start asking some questions again. Just like a good tool, this book is valuable only if you use it.

"On Dad's Life

**"We make a living by what we get;
we make a life by what we give."**
—Sir Winston Churchill

The questions in this section offer a glimpse into what Dad remembers as some of the highlights of his childhood and life. Consider this the ideal place to begin a conversation, offering Dad a listening ear and an interested mind. He's a wealth of stories and insights, and the more you learn, the more you'll remember. Plus, Dad will appreciate and enjoy the opportunity to share those special moments from his past and what's especially meaningful to him about his life.

As you and Dad reflect on his childhood, flash back to the time when he was a young boy. Discover what was important to him, what type of child he was, and how he was raised.

Like a puzzle, there will be many aspects of Dad's life that intersect. As he answers each question, try to keep him focused on that specific topic. There will be many questions to ask him that relate to a wide scope of themes as you continue.

Begin by sharing with Dad that these questions are an overview in many ways of his life, how he lived it, and the highlights. Stay centered on each question, asking him to share something specific as you progress. For example, if he starts talking about when he was in the fifth grade, there is probably a story or two that he can tell you. Was there one girl that he had a crush on? Did she know it? Or is there something in particular about that school that makes it memorable for him? Does he remember where his desk was in the classroom?

Pay special attention to his eyes and his facial expressions as he is talking with you about these items that are such an integral part of who he is, and who you are. You will probably see a sparkle in his eyes that you have not seen in a long time. Capture not only the words he is saying, but also the expressions he is using—not just the words but the hand motions, the way he lifts his head to the left and looks into space where all of those dear images are stored. Seal into your own memory bank the calm look on his face; that image could turn out to be one of your dearest memories of him.

Do you know how you got your name? Were there any special family relatives that you were named after?

_____

_____

_____

_____

_____

_____

_____

_____

_____

_____

_____

_____

Do you know any details about the time when you were born?

Can you share any of the earliest memories of your birthdays?

_ _

_ _

_ _

_ _

_ _

_ _

_ _

_ _

_ _

_ _

_ _

_ _

_ _

What are some of your earliest memories about your birthplace and growing up?

_____

_____

_____

_____

_____

_____

_____

_____

_____

_____

_____

_____

_____

If you could go back and visit where you grew up, what is one place you'd like to visit and see again? Who is the one person you'd like to see and visit with?

_____

_____

_____

_____

_____

_____

_____

_____

_____

_____

_____

Who were some of your childhood friends, and what special memories do you recall about the times you shared with them? Do you stay in touch with any of these friends? If so, who are they, and can you tell me how that makes you feel?

_____

_____

_____

_____

_____

_____

_____

_____

_____

_____

_____

How did others describe you when you were a young boy?

_____

_____

_____

_____

_____

_____

_____

_____

_____

_____

_____

_____

Did you have any special chores that you did as a child?
What was your least favorite one?

_____

_____

_____

_____

_____

_____

_____

_____

_____

_____

_____

_____

_____

Was there anything you were given as a child that became one of your prized possessions?

_____

_____

_____

_____

_____

_____

_____

_____

_____

_____

_____

_____

Did you feel that you had to do without anything when you were young? What was it?

_____

_____

_____

_____

_____

_____

_____

_____

_____

_____

_____

_____

_____

Do you have any special memories of family dinnertime as you were growing up? What are those memories?

_____

_____

_____

_____

_____

_____

_____

_____

_____

_____

_____

_____

_____

What was your favorite neighborhood place to play as a youngster?

_____

_____

_____

_____

_____

_____

_____

_____

_____

_____

_____

_____

_____

What hobbies did you enjoy during your youth? What hobbies and things do you now enjoy most as an adult?

_____

_____

_____

_____

_____

_____

_____

_____

_____

_____

_____

_____

_____

What were you good at as a child? What weren't you good at?

_____

_____

_____

_____

_____

_____

_____

_____

_____

_____

_____

_____

_____

What accomplishment in your life are you proudest of?

_____

_____

_____

_____

_____

_____

_____

_____

_____

_____

_____

_____

Is there anything you have done in your life that you regret?

_____

_____

_____

_____

_____

_____

_____

_____

_____

_____

_____

_____

_____

" On Our Family History "

"The family is the nucleus of civilization."
—William James Durant

Dad's family history helped shape him into the man he is today. The following questions are very important, for they pay a loving tribute to his life, including his parents and family. Dad's family history also impacts your life and your children's lives, so pay attention to the little details that you learn along the way.

This section contains questions you can ask your dad about his family and the things they did when he was younger. This also gives you a chance to gain a better understanding of why he is the way he is. You might not like everything you hear or read, but all of it is a part of the makeup of who you are.

When you hear or read something about your family history that you did not already know, try asking a probing question to learn even more about it—to get beyond the superficial answer. For example, if your dad says that their favorite vacation spot when he was young was a cabin in a particular campground, you might try to find out why. Was it close to the house, or was it far away? Did they go there because it did not cost much to go camping, or were there other reasons why they chose that?

When you start to write down the information you want to pass along to *your* children, this section on your dad's family history will be very important. This is where your children will find out about their grandpa and other relatives who were rarely seen. This section can really be fun because you are able to learn so much more about other members of the family tree—those aunts and uncles, and maybe even your grandparents, whom you saw occasionally but did not spend a lot of time with.

Depending on the family dynamics in your dad's life, this section might be a little touchy. If this is the case, we suggest that you save this section until after you have already talked with your dad on several other sections. By starting in some of the easier sections, you will be able to establish a rapport that becomes more conversational rather than just an interviewing situation. Once you have developed the kind of bond that allows you to ask almost anything, then you can come back to this section.

Is there anything you wish you could have asked your dad but never got around to?

_____

_____

_____

_____

_____

_____

_____

_____

_____

_____

_____

_____

What would you like future generations to know about your parents?

_____

_____

_____

_____

_____

_____

_____

_____

_____

_____

_____

_____

_____

What would you like future generations to know about your grandparents and our family history?

_____

_____

_____

_____

_____

_____

_____

_____

_____

_____

_____

_____

_____

What was the best advice your dad gave you when you were younger that has always stayed on your mind?

_____

_____

_____

_____

_____

_____

_____

_____

_____

_____

_____

_____

_____

What was the best advice your mom gave you when you were younger that has always stayed on your mind?

_____

_____

_____

_____

_____

_____

_____

_____

_____

_____

_____

_____

Can you share what you loved most about your father?

_____

_____

_____

_____

_____

_____

_____

_____

_____

_____

_____

_____

_____

Can you share one story about him that you would want passed on to the next generation?

_____

_____

_____

_____

_____

_____

_____

_____

_____

_____

_____

_____

_____

Can you share what you loved most about your mother? What is one memory of her that makes you feel special as her son?

_____

_____

_____

_____

_____

_____

_____

_____

_____

_____

_____

_____

_____

Can you share any special traditions, gatherings, or family get-togethers that you particularly remember?

_____

_____

_____

_____

_____

_____

_____

_____

_____

_____

_____

_____

_____

_____

What traditions that are important to you do you wish we'd continue, and why?

_____

_____

_____

_____

_____

_____

_____

_____

_____

_____

_____

_____

_____

What traditions did you share with your extended family?

_____

_____

_____

_____

_____

_____

_____

_____

_____

_____

_____

_____

_____

How did you get along with your brothers and sisters? If you are an only child, were there special friends who seemed like a brother or a sister to you? What special stories do you remember about them?

_____

_____

_____

_____

_____

_____

_____

_____

_____

_____

_____

_____

What family member did you most look up to and want to be like?

_____

_____

_____

_____

_____

_____

_____

_____

_____

_____

_____

_____

What family member was the most interesting? Why did he or she fascinate you?

_____

_____

_____

_____

_____

_____

_____

_____

_____

_____

_____

_____

Do you have a favorite family photograph that you could show me and tell me all about? Why is that photograph special to you?

_____

_____

_____

_____

_____

_____

_____

_____

_____

_____

_____

_____

What do you think made our family special that you hope is carried on by the next generation?

_____

_____

_____

_____

_____

_____

_____

_____

_____

_____

_____

_____

_____

"On Dad's Values

> **"Try not to become a man of success.
> Rather become a man of value."**
> —Albert Einstein

This section focuses on Dad's values. These are the beliefs your dad lives his life by and that challenge you as well to be the best person you can be. Values inspire us to do the right thing, and when we do, we honor the core values that a good life is based on. As you ask Dad about the principles that he cares most about, consider your own values. Did you learn them from Dad? Did he encourage you to live your life by these guiding thoughts and ideals? Are you following along the path that you know you should? It's not easy to do, but an honest, open reflection on your dad's beliefs might help you when you face times that require some serious soul-searching.

Many people automatically connect having values to being religious. There certainly can be a connection there, but everyone can have values in their life, and we know that not everyone is religious. Our values are the core of what and who we are. Have you ever been in a situation where you could have gotten away with something, but you chose the honorable way? Why did you make the right choice? Were you afraid that someone might see you, and you would then feel guilty? Or did you do the right thing just because it was the right thing to do? Did you learn your values from Dad?

Most of us are products of our environments, and it would be very natural for your values to mirror those of your dad. After you have the answers to these questions about Dad, think how you would answer the same questions. Are the answers the same? Are they at least similar? What do you think could be the reason if the answers are vastly different?

A valid question that you might want to ask us is this: "But what if my dad's values are *not* the ones that I really want to mirror?" We do not want to do any preaching in this book about moral judgments or what is right and what is wrong. You're a grownup, and you can make those choices for yourself.

What one or two things would you want me to be certain of, to know, or to understand as I go through life?

_____

_____

_____

_____

_____

_____

_____

_____

_____

_____

_____

_____

Are you afraid of dying? What is it that you fear most? What will you miss the most?

_____

_____

_____

_____

_____

_____

_____

_____

_____

_____

_____

_____

_____

Has your faith ever been tested? How did you handle it? What advice do you have for me?

_____

_____

_____

_____

_____

_____

_____

_____

_____

_____

_____

_____

How do you handle life when things feel overwhelming?

_____

_____

_____

_____

_____

_____

_____

_____

_____

_____

_____

_____

How do you handle disappointment? What example can you give
me so that I can be better prepared when I have to face it?

_____

_____

_____

_____

_____

_____

_____

_____

_____

_____

_____

_____

Can you share your memories of a time when you spoke up for someone and did a good deed?

_____

_____

_____

_____

_____

_____

_____

_____

_____

_____

_____

_____

_____

Can you share a motto you have lived your life by, or a good deed you have performed that gave you the greatest satisfaction? What was your inspiration at the time?

_____

_____

_____

_____

_____

_____

_____

_____

_____

_____

_____

_____

What do you value most when it comes to friends, and what kind of a friend are you to others?

_____

_____

_____

_____

_____

_____

_____

_____

_____

_____

_____

_____

_____

Who are your friends—the ones you can count on and who would be there no matter what?

_____

_____

_____

_____

_____

_____

_____

_____

_____

_____

_____

_____

If you could change one thing about yourself, what would it be? What insight can you share about why you would want to make that change?

What moral dilemmas have you faced? What did you rely upon to get through them?

_____

_____

_____

_____

_____

_____

_____

_____

_____

_____

_____

_____

_____

What has been your basis for handling peer pressure—both as a youth and as an adult?

_____

_____

_____

_____

_____

_____

_____

_____

_____

_____

_____

_____

_____

_____

On Marriage and Relationships

"One should believe in marriage as in the immortality of the soul."
—Honoré de Balzac

The topic of love, marriage, and relationships is certainly an important one. Approach these questions with care. Some dads are willing to address these topics freely while others, not as open, are more reserved about addressing their relationships. Depending on the nature of your family structure, you might consider including your mom in these discussions, if that is possible.

Consider what's important in this section for you to accomplish. What do you really want to know? What might help you later in life as you deal with relationship issues or otherwise? Perhaps you want to better understand Dad's feelings and these questions will give you a glance into his heart and what matters most to him.

We know that some people have parents who are divorced or separated for various reasons. That does not mean that you should not ask these questions. You may have to approach Dad in a slightly different manner, but it still very important to know his feelings. After you and he have worked through several of the "easier" sections, you could say something like this: "Dad, we are now coming to some questions that might seem a bit awkward given the circumstances. But I know you must have cared a lot about Mom when you married her. Those are the feelings I want to know about. Those are the memories I hope you can share with me."

You are asking him to address some issues that are probably difficult for him, especially if he is on the stubborn side. Don't press him if he is not ready to answer these questions right now.

In addition to marriage, does your dad have other relationships that have been formed over the years? Are there people from work, or around the neighborhood, with whom he seems to enjoy spending time? Does he like to visit certain people when he travels? As you find out more about these other people in your dad's life, you will learn more about how he values relationships. You will also gain more insight into the reasons that your family is the way it is, as well as some of the dynamics that took place over many years.

What were your hopes and dreams for your children when it comes to marriage? What advice do you think I should give my children before they get married?

_____

_____

_____

_____

_____

_____

_____

_____

_____

_____

_____

_____

How did you first meet Mom? What were your first thoughts? Was it love at first sight?

_____

_____

_____

_____

_____

_____

_____

_____

_____

_____

_____

_____

What can you share about your first date?

_____

_____

_____

_____

_____

_____

_____

_____

_____

_____

_____

_____

What is it about Mom that makes you love her so much?

_____

_____

_____

_____

_____

_____

_____

_____

_____

_____

_____

_____

_____

How have you and Mom learned to deal with your differences?

_____

_____

_____

_____

_____

_____

_____

_____

_____

_____

_____

_____

When did you know that you wanted to marry Mom? How did you propose to her?

_____

_____

_____

_____

_____

_____

_____

_____

_____

_____

_____

_____

_____

Have you ever doubted your marriage? What was it that caused you to have doubts?

_____

_____

_____

_____

_____

_____

_____

_____

_____

_____

_____

_____

_____

[If your dad was married more than once] How come your first marriage didn't last? When did you first feel that it was in trouble?

What do you wish you knew then that you know now about relationships, in life and in love?

_____

_____

_____

_____

_____

_____

_____

_____

_____

_____

_____

_____

Who has mentored you in your life? Is it someone you value outside the family?

_____

_____

_____

_____

_____

_____

_____

_____

_____

_____

_____

_____

_____

"On Dad's Dreams and Goals"

"A goal is a dream with a deadline."
—Harvey Mackay

All dads hope for the future to be bright, happy, and prosperous, especially when it comes to providing for their families. The future of your dad's loved ones is his waking concern—that those things he worked for and hoped for would become a reality. Search for the lessons he learned along the way, and encourage a conversation that will offer you insight into how your dad overcame adversity, rose to the occasion during difficult times, and not just obtained success, but also accomplished what he had always hoped for.

As he is answering these questions, try to dig deeper for more information. How was he feeling at the time? Did he absolutely know he was going to be successful? Who was giving him the encouragement he needed? What might have been the consequences if he had not succeeded? These follow-up questions will give you additional insight that you can use when you are addressing similar situations. Share with Dad your own hopes and dreams, for you will discover that your success is ultimately his greatest accomplishment as well. He might even be willing to offer you some guidance on how he would have handled the situations you are facing.

Your dad's generation was brought up with different goals than most of us have today—they had come through hard times (depressions, wars, recessions). So it is not unusual if some of their goals might seem simple to you. Do not discount the fact that a primary motivator in your dad's life might have been to see you go to college, or for him to be able to retire and play golf several times a week. What might seem like a given to you could have been a stretch for your dad. Let him know how much you appreciate the sacrifices he made so that you could have an easier life.

Once again, if there is any one section where you do not want to be judgmental, this is it. If your dad's dreams and goals sound mundane to you, try to put yourself in his position when he was your age—did he have any luxuries that you now consider necessities? Was he living at home while going to school, or was he working two jobs? If you want to feel humble, put yourself in your dad's shoes and see how well you would do in the same situation.

What did you want to be when you were a little boy?

_____

_____

_____

_____

_____

_____

_____

_____

_____

_____

_____

_____

_____

When you were a young boy, was there any particular job or career that you envisioned yourself doing when you grew up? What attracted you to that?

_____

_____

_____

_____

_____

_____

_____

_____

_____

_____

_____

_____

What is your greatest accomplishment in life? What would have been your answer ten years ago? Twenty years ago?

_____

_____

_____

_____

_____

_____

_____

_____

_____

_____

_____

_____

What is one dream you have not made come true yet, but you hope one day to make happen?

If you ever wrote a book, what would it be about?

_____

_____

_____

_____

_____

_____

_____

_____

_____

_____

_____

_____

_____

Can you share a time that you were disappointed because one of your goals or dreams did not come true, but you rose above it?

_____

_____

_____

_____

_____

_____

_____

_____

_____

_____

_____

How did you go about resetting your goal or your dream?

_____

_____

_____

_____

_____

_____

_____

_____

_____

_____

_____

_____

_____

Do you have any regrets in life, things that you wished you had done differently? Is it too late to do them now?

_____

_____

_____

_____

_____

_____

_____

_____

_____

_____

_____

_____

_____

What goals do you think you might have if you were my age today? How different are they from the goals you had when you were my age? What makes them different?

_____

_____

_____

_____

_____

_____

_____

_____

_____

_____

_____

_____

What has been your main source of motivation? When did that start?

_____

_____

_____

_____

_____

_____

_____

_____

_____

_____

_____

_____

_____

Do you listen to, or have you listened to, inspirational tapes or CDs?
How do they inspire you; how long does that inspiration burst last?

_____

_____

_____

_____

_____

_____

_____

_____

_____

_____

_____

_____

Do you keep a written list of your goals? What do you do to keep them fresh in your mind?

_____

_____

_____

_____

_____

_____

_____

_____

_____

_____

_____

_____

What book or books would you recommend that I read one day?

_____

_____

_____

_____

_____

_____

_____

_____

_____

_____

_____

_____

_____

Do you have a favorite movie that inspired you?

_____

_____

_____

_____

_____

_____

_____

_____

_____

_____

_____

_____

_____

On Parenting
and Children

"It is a wise father that knows his own child."
—William Shakespeare

Being a father is a full-time job. From supporting a family to raising children, a father's responsibilities are often the core of his existence. This selection of questions focuses on the type of dad your father is or was. It's a wonderful opportunity to let Dad know what he did that helped you grow up into the person you are today. This is not to take anything at all away from everything that your mom did—most of what she did was probably more visible than your dad's contribution, and both of them worked hard to give you the life that you had.

Once you become a parent, you also appreciate your own parents more than ever. It's a huge job and one of the most rewarding ones in life. The questions in this section will help you learn a great deal about your parents' joy when you were born. Here are the little details that fade over time, from the day you were born to how your father and/or mother selected your name. This is an especially wonderful chapter since it's your heritage that Dad will address.

As your dad talks about you when you were very young, he might get a little off-track in his conversation—allow him that freedom. In fact, you can probably use this side conversation to find out even more about him. If he mentions anything about the house where you lived back then, ask about the neighbors. Were they close friends? Did the families do things together? Even if there are not specific questions in this book along these lines, this allows your dad more freedom to talk about his wonderful memories.

If you are already a parent, then this chapter will have an extra special meaning. Ask your dad questions that will help you be the best parent you can be. Think about your own parenting style— what have you learned from your father that you are passing down to your children? Use this section as a catalyst to gain clarity about what matters most to you, and then consider how it affects your own children. If you see some characteristics in your dad as a parent that you do not want to pass on to your children, keep that to yourself. This is another area where it might be easy to judge your dad (and your mom) on the way you were brought up—please don't. See what lessons you can take from those experiences, and made the necessary adjustments in your own role as a parent.

How did you and Mom decide on my name and its spelling? Did you use books to look up names, or did you want to use a name that was special to you? How far in advance did you agree on my name?

_____

_____

_____

_____

_____

_____

_____

_____

_____

_____

_____

_____

Can you share any details about the day I was born? What was the weather like? Was there a lot of traffic as you drove to the hospital?

_____

_____

_____

_____

_____

_____

_____

_____

_____

_____

_____

_____

How did life change for you when I was born?

_____

_____

_____

_____

_____

_____

_____

_____

_____

_____

_____

_____

Can you think of a time when I was a baby that you were taking care of me or we did something special?

_____

_____

_____

_____

_____

_____

_____

_____

_____

_____

_____

_____

_____

What did I do that drove you crazy when I was a toddler?

_____

_____

_____

_____

_____

_____

_____

_____

_____

_____

_____

_____

What is one thing I have done that has made you proud of me?

_____

_____

_____

_____

_____

_____

_____

_____

_____

_____

_____

_____

How do you manage to unconditionally love your children, no matter what?

_____

_____

_____

_____

_____

_____

_____

_____

_____

_____

_____

_____

What weren't you great at when I was little?

_____

_____

_____

_____

_____

_____

_____

_____

_____

_____

_____

_____

_____

What did you teach me to do when I was younger that you were proud of?

_____

_____

_____

_____

_____

_____

_____

_____

_____

_____

_____

_____

_____

What activities did you love to share with me? Was there a time that you recall was memorable?

_____

_____

_____

_____

_____

_____

_____

_____

_____

_____

_____

_____

_____

If you were to give me one piece of advice based on what you have learned as a father that I should know and pass down to my children, what would it be?

_____

_____

_____

_____

_____

_____

_____

_____

_____

_____

_____

_____

Do you think it was harder to raise children when I was young than it is today?

_____

_____

_____

_____

_____

_____

_____

_____

_____

_____

_____

_____

_____

What were some of the things you had to do then that are taken for granted today when raising a child?

_____

_____

_____

_____

_____

_____

_____

_____

_____

_____

_____

_____

How did you maintain sanity when you worked and then came home to a noisy household?

_____

_____

_____

_____

_____

_____

_____

_____

_____

_____

_____

_____

Would you have wished for more children? Why? Why didn't you have more?

_____

_____

_____

_____

_____

_____

_____

_____

_____

_____

_____

_____

How did we behave as children compared to the neighbors and their children?

_____

_____

_____

_____

_____

_____

_____

_____

_____

_____

_____

_____

_____

On Dad's Vision
for His Children

> "I hope your vision for your children is not for them to be professional athletes. Having had that as a personal goal when I was in high school and college, I can attest to the fact that all that glitters isn't gold."
> —Norm Wakefield

The previous section focused on your dad's role as a parent in terms of raising you from an infant to where you are today. This section is about the dreams and visions and plans that he had (or maybe still has) for a better life for you. That better life could be in terms of education, career, or opportunities to travel, meet new people, and see new things.

There is also a natural force in parents that compels them to want to see you succeed. How many times has your dad told you, "You can do better than that"? Do you think he pushed you harder just so you couldn't have any fun? Or do you think it was so you could reach your potential?

The questions in this section are a combination of learning more about your dad as well as learning more about yourself—at different stages in your life—from his perspective. Just as we cannot know exactly what it is like to be someone else, you might be surprised to hear your dad's view of certain things about you. Unless he is intentionally trying to distort the facts, his descriptions might still be a little different from what you remember or perhaps what other people have told you about events from your childhood. That's okay—keep in mind that the reason you are asking him these questions is to get you closer to him in many ways.

You may sense a hint of frustration as your dad begins to answer some of these questions. The reason for the apparent frustration is that he always wanted you to do better—make better grades, run faster, jump higher. This will be the case in all dads. Use those times when he says things like, "But you could have done better" to ask what he thought you should have done to "do better." Reassure him that you were trying to do your best (assuming that you were), and that it wasn't a matter of not wanting to listen to him.

What was the one main thing that you wanted me to be better at than you were?

_____

_____

_____

_____

_____

_____

_____

_____

_____

_____

_____

_____

Was there a career you thought I'd be perfect for as I was growing up?

_____

_____

_____

_____

_____

_____

_____

_____

_____

_____

_____

_____

_____

What have you learned about working that you hope I know?

_____

_____

_____

_____

_____

_____

_____

_____

_____

_____

_____

_____

_____

Where did you want me to go to school, and what did you want me to study? Why?

_____

_____

_____

_____

_____

_____

_____

_____

_____

_____

_____

_____

_____

Were there times when my accomplishments did not match your expectations? What can you tell me about those times?

_____

_____

_____

_____

_____

_____

_____

_____

_____

_____

_____

_____

What was the best way that you found to motivate me? Why do you think that worked better than other ways?

_____

_____

_____

_____

_____

_____

_____

_____

_____

_____

_____

_____

Do you still have some dreams and aspirations for me? What are they?

_____

_____

_____

_____

_____

_____

_____

_____

_____

_____

_____

_____

If I do one thing really well in life, what do you think that should be?

_____

_____

_____

_____

_____

_____

_____

_____

_____

_____

_____

_____

How do you think we're alike? How do you think we're different?

_____

_____

_____

_____

_____

_____

_____

_____

_____

_____

_____

_____

_____

What part of our relationship do you wish we could work on?

_____

_____

_____

_____

_____

_____

_____

_____

_____

_____

_____

_____

"On Dad's Legacy"

"The legacy we leave is not just in our possessions, but in the quality of our lives."

—Billy Graham

This section contains questions you can ask your dad about the things he wants people to remember about him. When you think about your dad, it is important to know his thoughts, his feelings, his likes, his dislikes—all the things that make him unique and that he wants people to hold on to and not forget.

None of us lives forever, but that does not mean that this section has to focus on our mortality. As you are asking these questions, try to focus on the things that are truly "Dad." As you look at a question, go beyond the simple one- or two-sentence answer. Expand on the answer with an example of something your dad did that made it very memorable—for him or for you. If your dad wanted to be known for being able to make almost anything out of a block of wood, take it an extra step and find out if there were ever any times when something funny happened as he was working on a project. Or perhaps he was just about done, and the saw slipped and cut it in half—and he had to start all over. Try to find that extra dimension in the answers that is not always offered out right away. Those are the stories that are fun to pass along.

Keep these thoughts in mind as you are talking with your dad about this section. You may have other thoughts, and that's okay. We want to offer these as a guiding path in case you need one.

- Throughout your life, your dad's love has brightened your world. A life without his physical presence might seem unbearable and impossible, but sadly, one day, that will become a reality.
- This section is devoted to helping Dad craft the future—from what he wants you to remember, to his words he hopes you'll hear.
- Honor his life by celebrating what he cared about believing in and more.
- Let Dad's legacy be based on love, and instill in your heart his words of wisdom and your insights into his life.
- This is the time to make sure that you have everything you need to preserve his legacy today so you have no regrets tomorrow.

What is the one main thing you would want to say to your family before you die?

_____

_____

_____

_____

_____

_____

_____

_____

_____

_____

_____

_____

How do you want to be remembered?

_____

_____

_____

_____

_____

_____

_____

_____

_____

_____

_____

_____

_____

What specific things do you want us to do when you pass away?

_____

_____

_____

_____

_____

_____

_____

_____

_____

_____

_____

_____

If you were to describe the perfect funeral, what would it look like? Who would you want to give your eulogy? What would you want them to say?

_____

_____

_____

_____

_____

_____

_____

_____

_____

_____

_____

_____

One day, when I am describing you to future generations, what would you want me to share about you?

_____

_____

_____

_____

_____

_____

_____

_____

_____

_____

_____

_____

_____

What possessions would you want us to keep and pass down?
Why are those things important to you?

_____

_____

_____

_____

_____

_____

_____

_____

_____

_____

_____

_____

_____

What pictures of you should I hold most dear? What memories do they bring to you?

_____

_____

_____

_____

_____

_____

_____

_____

_____

_____

_____

_____

_____

What are some key words that you want me to always remember?
What special thoughts and feelings do they evoke for you?

_ _

_ _

_ _

_ _

_ _

_ _

_ _

_ _

_ _

_ _

_ _

_ _

_ _

"Who Knows Dad Best?"

This section is especially important if you want to learn about your dad through the eyes of others. It is very helpful if your dad is modest, won't say much, or perhaps is even deceased. Consider the amount of time your dad has spent with friends, other family members, and coworkers. This is your chance to ask these people about their favorite memories of your dad, and their feelings about him, and to preserve those memories that perhaps would be forgotten.

For those whose dad is no longer with them, you will actually be doing a favor for those whom you contact. They will feel special because you have taken the time to ask them about your dad. There may be some tears shed as they tell you why he was so special. Think of those tears, and the ones you shed, as being the glue that ties all those special memories together.

There are two sets of Who Knows Dad Best questions, but you can photocopy these pages to ask more than two people the questions.

Who Knows Dad Best

When did you meet my dad and how?

_____

_____

_____

_____

What did you think of him when you first met him?

_____

_____

_____

_____

What are some of the most special memories you have of him?

_____

_____

_____

_____

If you had to sum up my dad in one word, what would that be? Why did you choose that word?

_____

_____

_____

_____

Is there anything my dad taught you that inspired you and that you recall to this day?

_____

_____

_____

_____

Was there a time when my dad helped you in any way?

_____

_____

_____

_____

How well did you know him, and how did it change your relationship?

_____

_____

_____

_____

What do you think was important to my dad?

_____

_____

_____

_____

What do you think my dad did best?

_____

_____

_____

_____

What were his strengths?

_____

_____

_____

_____

What were some of my dad's weaknesses?

_____

_____

_____

_____

Was there a time when my dad was stubborn?

_____

_____

_____

_____

Is there anything you wish my dad didn't do or could have done better?

_____

_____

_____

If you were to describe your favorite things about my dad, what would they be?

_____

_____

_____

Is there any other special memory you have of my dad?

_____

_____

_____

Who Knows Dad Best

When did you meet my dad and how?

_ _

_ _

_ _

_ _

What did you think of him when you first met him?

_ _

_ _

_ _

_ _

What are some of the most special memories you have of him?

_ _

_ _

_ _

_ _

If you had to sum up my dad in one word, what would that be? Why did you choose that word?

_____

_____

_____

_____

Is there anything my dad taught you that inspired you and you recall to this day?

_____

_____

_____

_____

Was there a time when my dad helped you in any way?

_____

_____

_____

_____

How well did you know him, and how did it change your
relationship?

_____

_____

_____

_____

What do you think was important to my dad?

_____

_____

_____

_____

What do you think my dad did best?

_____

_____

_____

_____

What were his strengths?

_____

_____

_____

_____

What were some of my dad's weaknesses?

_____

_____

_____

_____

Was there a time when my dad was stubborn?

_____

_____

_____

_____

Is there anything you wish my dad didn't do or could have done better?

_____

_____

_____

_____

If you were to describe your favorite things about my dad, what would they be?

_____

_____

_____

_____

Is there any other special memory you have of my dad?

_____

_____

_____

_____

Miscellaneous notes about my dad

" Dad's Favorite Things "

From Dad's favorite foods, to movies, to places to travel, this section is a special reminder of Dad's favorite pastimes. Exploring each one of these areas will be like opening up a treasure chest. Your dad will certainly have a story or two to tell—if you ask for more information—about each of these. For example, don't just stop once he tells you the name of his favorite restaurant. Ask him more. Why does he like it so much? Was there one time that was more special than any other? Is that restaurant where he likes to go for very special occasions? Do the waiters know him by name? You can do a similar type of additional exploration for each of the questions. Have fun exploring!

If your dad is no longer with you, you can still fill out this section by asking other family members and friends. They will be happy to help you on your journey—asking them will also help them remember your dad one more time. That will be a treat for them.

Leisure Time
Favorite hobby:

_____

_____

Favorite holiday:

_____

_____

Favorite way to pass the time:

_____

_____

Good Eats
Favorite food for breakfast:

_____

_____

Favorite food for lunch:

_____

_____

Favorite food for dinner:

_ _

_ _

_ _

_ _

Favorite meal to make:

_ _

_ _

_ _

_ _

Least favorite food:

_ _

_ _

_ _

_ _

Favorite restaurant:

_____

_____

_____

_____

People, Places, and Entertainment
Person(s) you most admire:

_____

_____

_____

_____

Best advice you were ever given:

_____

_____

_____

_____

Special people/contacts Dad wants his family to know:

_____

_____

_____

_____

Favorite place(s) for a vacation:

_____

_____

_____

_____

Favorite movies:

_____

_____

_____

_____

Favorite movie stars:

_____

_____

_____

_____

Favorite television shows when you were younger:

_____

_____

_____

_____

Favorite television shows now:

_____

_____

_____

_____

Around the World with Dad

Places Dad has visited:

_____

_____

_____

Friends Dad made while traveling:

_____

_____

_____

Memories from Dad's favorite cities:

_____

_____

_____

Trips that were extra special:

_____

_____

"A Few Final Words"

We hope that you have found this book to be very helpful. We know that not every relationship between a child (of any age) and his or her dad is the ideal relationship, but there is a special bond that will always exist between them. Whether you used this book to learn more about your dad or you are the dad passing on information to your children, the thoughts and discussions you had alone or with others will also become a significant part of the shared memories. If this book has helped you to have more family discussions, please leverage that and have more family discussions—even the casual ones will have a more special meaning to all of you.

Make the most of it. Before the day ends, tell someone in your family, "I love you," and continue to share the words that were lovingly recorded in the pages of this very special book. Keep in mind that time is a memory we must store in our hearts. We feel certain that Dad would like that.

Stuart Gustafson is an author, mathematician, computer scientist, and university professor whose own father died before he could ask these vital questions. This book is his effort to give readers what he could not give himself. He lives in Boise, Idaho.

Robyn Freedman Spizman is an award-winning author who has written dozens of inspirational and educational nonfiction books during her career, including *Make It Memorable*, *When Words Matter Most*, *GIFTionary*, and *The Thank You Book*. She also coauthored the Women for Hire series (with Tory Johnson) and debuted her first novel for young readers, *Secret Agent* (with Mark Johnston). As a seasoned media personality and consumer advocate for more than twenty-three years, she has appeared often on NBC's *Today* and CNN and is featured regularly on the NBC Atlanta affiliate WXIA and Star 94. In addition to her writing, reporting, and speaking, she is also the cofounder of The Spizman Agency, a highly successful public relations firm that specializes in experts and book publicity. Visit *www.robynspizman.com* for more information. She lives in Atlanta, GA.